# Securely Rooted

# Securely Rooted

ROOTED AND GROUNDED
IN GOD'S LOVE

*Rodney Fortin*

www.resoundingword.org

For more information regarding permissions to reproduce materials of this book, please email or write:

Rodney Fortin
General Delivery
Drayton Valley, Alberta Canada
T7A1T1
www.resoundingword.org

"Scripture quotations taken from the New American Standard Bible® (NASB), Copyright © 1960, 1962, 1963, 1968, 1971, 1972, 1973, 1975, 1977, 1995 by The Lockman Foundation Used by permission. www.Lockman.org"

ISBN-13: 9781542373050
ISBN-10: 1542373050
Library of Congress Control Number: 2017900542
CreateSpace Independent Publishing Platform
North Charleston, South Carolina

# Dedication

*I would like to dedicate this book to:*

*My God, who always enriches my life, with every good and perfect gift. He has rooted and grounded me in His love, through His perfect son, Jesus Christ, through whom I have been brought into son-ship and have become an heir in Him.*

*My beloved wife Tracy, the love of my life, and my best friend who has always been a constant, invaluable help and support in my life and ministry.*

*My beloved children, Graham and Rachel, both of whom I deeply love, who have come along with us for the ride, often without knowing where the journey leads.*

# Contents

# Endorsements

"THE INSIGHTFUL USE OF SCRIPTURE is a reflection of Rodney's knowledge, the content of the text is a revelation of his heart. This book is a very enjoyable and inspirational read that continues to remind us that a fruitful Christian life is formed from the inside out. The personal testimonies confirm that these are not just words to him but are outward expressions of a deep-rooted relationship with the Lord. There are pages of practical how-to principles contained within this book and accompanying study guide that will help lay a solid foundation for the new believers and provide inspiration to the old. This is a recommended read! Well done Rodney!"

**Pastor Gary W. Carter**
**Founding Apostle of Life Church International**

"What a great book! Here we find the true revelation of the finished work of Christ made so simple. Too often we struggle in our Christian walk trying to be good enough or to be acceptable to God yet never really come to the place of fulfillment. Securely Rooted brings together all what seems to take so much energy and striving by revealing the Grace of God. God bless you Rodney and thank you for putting this material together. I'm convinced that many will be helped and rooted in Christ."

**Pastor Louw Ronquest**
**Senior Pastor Spirit Ablaze Ministries**

I am so happy to be able to endorse Rodney Fortin as a man whose passionate desire for God has always been obvious. His book 'Deeply Rooted' is evidence of that passion and reveals something of his own journey with God. I pray the wisdom, faith and truth expressed here will empower and inspire you to deepen your hold of God as you allow His hold on you to be 'Securely Rooted' in you.

Blessings,

*Marc Brisebois*
**Executive Director, *Watchman on the Wall***

God desires all people to be saved and come to the knowledge of the truth 1 Timothy 2:4. In Securely Rooted Rodney reveals how to move beyond salvation, from judgement, to learning how to function as a favored and mature son of God. He brings insight into how to move past basic feelings and fears into faith about the believers true identity and privilege. I highly recommend this book to anyone seeking to mature in their walk with Christ.

**Christopher Scarinzi**
**Apostolic leader, United With Christ Churches and Ministries**

# Preface

OVER THE LAST COUPLE OF years, I have watched my son and daughter move from adolescence into adulthood. They have both come into the season where curiosity in the opposite gender seems to have been awakened, and they have begun to take an interest. This new interest is, thankfully, completely innocent and awkward and you can see this in their interactions. As parents looking on, we know that the day is coming when we will have to let go, but for now there is a strong caution even within the confines of their innocence, to encourage them to exercise discernment and restraint until the time is right. There is a perfect time for everything, and God knows how to order our steps just right, and in His time. Solomon writes:

> "I adjure you, O daughters of Jerusalem, by the
> gazelles or by the hinds of the field, that you do
> not arouse or awaken my love until she pleases."

Song of Solomon 2:7 (NLT)

It is true, that we may not be ready at this time to encourage love to be awakened in our children. For God and His children, however, His timing is unfolding, for us who believe, where He is awaking the love that He has purposed for us, in Christ, from the beginning of creation. Before the foundation of the world, God desired to have someone who could share in the divine fellowship that was already self-existent within the eternal heavens between Father, Son and Holy Spirit. His move to fashion a man after His image and likeness was not to be taken lightly, as God was to let His glory shine on the crown of His creation in a splendorous display, as never before seen.

Forming man out of the dust of the earth, God made an earthen vessel; fragile and yet strong in stature, carrying the very essence of the Almighty. He then moved close enough to breathe into his nostrils the breath of life, making the man a living soul. Take a step back for a moment and just think of the significance of such intimacy. Just imagine the self-existent Creator of the universe, one having no beginning or end of days, the God who flung the stars into their place, positioned Himself in close enough proximity, to simply lean forward and breathe His life into a piece of clay.

> "Then the Lord God formed man of dust from the
> ground, and breathed into his nostrils the breath
> of life; and man became a living being."
>
> Genesis 2:7 (NASB)

This living being (soul) was to be set apart from all of the rest of the creation. God gave him a mind to think, reason and be creative like Himself. He gave man the ability to feel and express a range of emotions, both positive and negative. God also made man with a free will, with which he could make choices independently, which unfortunately, would eventually plunge him into darkness and eternal separation.

*"But your iniquities have made a separation between*
*you and your God, and your sins have hidden*
*His face from you so that He does not hear."*

*Isaiah 59:2 (NASB)*

Throughout the ages, God has been peeking out from time to time, just like the sun peeks out from behind the clouds. Glimpses of glory and a foreshadowing taste of divine love; stirring a hunger and thirst through the ages, until that glorious day when heaven erupted with a chorus of praise as God emptied Himself, and took on human form. He was born of a virgin, and heralded the Son of God. God chose the perfect time to send His Son, Jesus Christ, into the world, to begin the awakening that would allow love to take root in anyone who would receive Him as their Lord and Savior. The Apostle Paul wrote:

*"For this reason I bow my knees before the Father, from*
*whom every family in heaven and on earth derives*

*its name, that He would grant you, according to the*
*riches of His glory, to be strengthened with power*
*through His Spirit in the inner man, so that Christ*
*may dwell in your hearts through faith; and that you,*
*being rooted and grounded in love, may be able to*
*comprehend with all the saints what is the breadth*
*and length and height and depth, and to know the*
*love of Christ which surpasses knowledge, that you*
*may be filled up to all the fullness of God. "*

*Ephesians 3:14-19 (NASB)*

*"One of the world's best known children's songs is "Jesus Loves Me". Jesus loves me this I know for the bible tells me so Little ones to him belong they are weak but he is strong...*

*The song was originally composed for a novel, Say and Seal, published in 1860. It tells the story of a little boy, Johnny who is sick and dying. He is being rocked in the arms of his Sunday school teacher John Linden and asks John to sing him a song John sings "Jesus Loves Me".*

*The profundity of that song extends way beyond simplistic childhood faith. Karl Barth was one of the most influential theologians of the twentieth century. He possessed a brilliant mind and wrote thousands of words exploring the interrelation of faith, theology and culture. Towards the end of his life Barth gave a lecture at the University of Chicago Divinity*

*School. At the end of the lecture he was asked what he considered to be the greatest theological discovery of his life.*

*Everyone sat with bated breath ready for an extended and complex answer. Karl Barth paused for a moment, then smiled and said, "The greatest theological insight that I have ever had is this:*

*Jesus loves me, this I know, for the Bible tells me so!"*[1]

God's desire is that we would implant our roots and be grounded deep into the soil of God's love that we may be filled to the full measure of His glory. God has been stirring my heart with this message, and I am confident that it will propel you into a greater depth of what it means to be loved by God.

---

1 Reported in Deep Cove Crier, November 1993, Reporter Interactive (umr.org) May 2001 and Tony Campolo, Let Me Tell You a Story.

# CHAPTER 1
## Roots

A NUMBER OF YEARS AGO I was asked to help transplant a tree to a more suitable location in a friend's backyard. We anticipated an easy process, because the tree had only been there for a few years. To our surprise, the roots had dug themselves deeper into the ground than we had expected. We had much digging to do, by hand, to get under the existing root system to loosen its grip on the earth. The Bible declares that our lives are to be like this tree, in that we are not to be easily uprooted. The Apostle Paul gives us clear direction in how our lives should be rooted in the love of God:

> *"For this reason I bow my knees before the*
> *Father, from whom every family in heaven and*
> *on earth derives its name, that He would grant*
> *you, according to the riches of His glory, to be*
> *strengthened with power through His Spirit in*
> *the inner man, so that Christ may dwell in your*
> *hearts through faith; and that you, being rooted*

*and grounded in love, may be able to comprehend*
*with all the saints what is the breadth and*
*length and height and depth, and to know the*
*love of Christ which surpasses knowledge, that*
*you may be filled up to all the fullness of God."*

*Ephesians 3:14-19 (NASB)*

*Roots are the "part of a plant that attaches it to the ground or to a support, typically underground, conveying water and nourishment to the rest of the plant via numerous branches and fibers."[2]*

Using this simple definition of a root, we can see that the root is what sustains the tree with nourishment and stability. Francoise Du Toit speaks of the tree's root system being the love of God which is our invisible inner source.

*"Love is your invisible inner source just like the root system of a tree and the foundation of a building."[3]*

When we are well rooted and grounded in our faith, we have become strengthened in the reality of the love of God. This strength given to us by God is the epicenter of faith. The demonstrated evidence that love has taken root can be measured by the fullness of God in which we walk. Consider for a moment how you first received the Lord. The Apostle Paul writes:

---

2  Google Dictionary

3  Mirror Bible; François Du Toit

*"And hope does not disappoint, because **the love of*** ***God has been poured out within our hearts*** ***through the Holy Spirit*** *who was given to us."*

*Romans 5:5 (NASB)*

*"**Therefore as you have received Christ Jesus*** ***the Lord, so walk in Him, having been*** ***firmly rooted and now being built up in Him*** ***and established in your faith,*** *just as you were* *instructed, and overflowing with gratitude."*

*Colossians 2:6-7(NASB)*

*The definition of the Greek word used for "**rooted**" means;*

*"To become strengthened, with focus upon the source of such* *strength—'to be strengthened, to be rooted in."*[4]

Essentially what Paul is saying in both of these passages of scripture, is that when we are firmly rooted in the love of Christ, we draw strength from Him to walk in His fullness. The Apostle John writes:

---

4  Louw, J. P., & Nida, E. A. (1996). Greek-English lexicon of the New Testament: based on semantic domains (electronic ed. of the 2nd edition., Vol. 1, p. 677). New York: United Bible Societies.

> *"Abide in Me, and I in you. As **the branch cannot bear***
> ***fruit of itself unless it abides in the vine**, so neither*
> *can you unless you abide in Me. I am the vine, you are*
> *the branches; he who abides in Me and I in him, he bears*
> *much fruit, for **apart from Me you can do nothing.**"*

*John 15:4-5 (NASB)*

The Bible tells us that God placed us in Jesus Christ, and the primary reason for this extraordinary placement was so that we could come into maturity as sons of God and walk in His fullness. We exist solely for the purpose of bringing glory to the Father, and we can only accomplish this as we abide in the Lord Jesus; being rooted and grounded in Him, bearing fruit to the glory of the Father. According to the Apostle Paul, being rooted and grounded in love is the key to walking in God's fullness.

> *"that you, **being rooted and grounded in love**,*
> *may be able to comprehend with all the saints what is*
> *the width and length and depth and height—to know*
> *the love of Christ which passes knowledge; **that you***
> ***may be filled with all the fullness of God.**"*

*Ephesians 3:14-19 (NASB)*

There are key principles found in God's word that we will be exploring in depth, that will help us discover what it means to rightly know the love of Christ, allowing us to be firmly rooted and grounded.

Do you realize what God has deposited in you, through Christ? From the moment His life poured into your spirit you became strong and powerful, becoming fully able to manifest God's power. He poured out His Spirit so that we would be reinforced in our inner being with the resurrection life of Christ. The Apostle Paul knew the magnitude of what the fullness of God's unceasing love represented in our lives, and he expressed this in his letter to the Romans:

> *"Who will separate us from the love of Christ? Will tribulation, or distress, or persecution, or famine, or nakedness, or peril, or sword? Just as it is written,*

> *"For Your sake we are being put to death all day long; we were considered as sheep to be slaughtered."*

> *But in all these things we overwhelmingly conquer through Him who loved us. For **I am convinced** that **neither death, nor life, nor angels, nor principalities, nor things present, nor things to come, nor powers, nor height, nor depth, nor any other created thing, will be able to separate us from the love of God**, which is in Christ Jesus our Lord."*

> *Romans 8:35-39 (NASB)*

A couple of years ago, I was given what is called a Tefillin that the Jews bind on their arm and forehead as they were instructed to do so by Moses in the wilderness. One day as

I put it on, I received a very powerful revelation of God's inseparable love for us. I looked down in the center of my hand, and saw the wrap of the leather band that formed a little Hebrew letter when translated revealed the word "hand". What God showed me was this little hand bound to an even bigger hand. Tears began to stream down my face when I realized that my life was tied to His, and nothing could ever separate me from Him! Are you convinced that nothing can ever separate you from the love of God? God help us to see this incredible reality!

The Apostle Paul wanted to remind the church that they could never be separated from God's love. If there were even the remote possibility of this, we would be cut off from the very source that sustains our lives. God's love is how we will live move and have our being for all of eternity.

Allow me to speak to the issue of our hearts becoming the dwelling place of God. God wants to establish His permanent dwelling place in us, through Christ, by faith, in our innermost being. Looking back into Ephesians 3:17, t*he definition of the Greek word used for '***dwell***' means;*

> *"live or dwell in a place in an established or settled manner— to live, to dwell, to reside."*[5]

5 Louw, J. P., & Nida, E. A. (1996). Greek-English lexicon of the New Testament: based on semantic domains (electronic ed. of the 2nd edition., Vol. 1, p. 730). New York: United Bible Societies.

Theologian Wuest writes:

> *"that Christ might finally settle down and feel completely at home in your hearts." Dr. Max Reich once said in the hearing of the writer, "If we make room for the Holy Spirit, He will make room for the Lord Jesus."*[6]

Jesus wants His life to take root in our lives. He wants to become the nourishment and stability that we require in order to walk in our full kingdom potential. It is imperative, that we realize that our only source of strength is Jesus Christ, and the power of His Spirit in us.

> *"But if the Spirit of Him who raised Jesus from the dead dwells in you, **He who raised Christ Jesus from the dead will also give life to your mortal bodies through His Spirit who dwells in you.**"*

*Romans 8:11 (NASB)*

The Spirit of Christ is continuously reinforcing our inner being as we focus on Him.

---

6 Wuest, K. S. (1997). Wuest's word studies from the Greek New Testament: for the English reader (Eph. 3:17). Grand Rapids: Eerdmans.

> "but whenever a person turns to the Lord, the veil is taken away. Now the Lord is the Spirit, and where the Spirit of the Lord is, there is liberty. But **we all, with unveiled face, beholding as in a mirror the glory of the Lord, are being transformed into the same image from glory to glory,** just as from the Lord, the Spirit." *2 Corinthians 3:16-18 (NASB)*

Our transformation into the fullness of God is fully dependent upon our continued gaze upon the Lord Jesus Christ.

> "But the Helper, the Holy Spirit, whom the Father will send in My name, He will teach you all things, and bring to your remembrance all that I said to you."
>
> John 14:26 (NASB)

When the Holy Spirit reinforces our inner being, this is what will happen: Our faith will be ignited and we will walk in the realities of resurrection power.

Through the Spirit's empowerment, Christ can dwell in our hearts, enabling us to comprehend and rightly know His love, so that we can be filled with the fullness of God. Being rooted and grounded in love is the key, and this is the work Holy Spirit is doing in our lives so that we will know the love of God, unto fullness. In order to be rooted and grounded in love, we must begin to comprehend what love is.

It begins with God and this statement written by John the Apostle:

*"The one who does not love does not know God, for God is love."*

*I John 4:8 (NASB)*

It is not even possible to say that you know God apart from His love, because you could never separate Him from this absolute reality. Wuest suggests these words concerning the above statement:

*"The translation should read, "God as to His nature is love." That is, God is a loving God. It is His nature to be loving."[7]*

*Our response to a God whose nature is demonstrated as loving should naturally be to manifest itself in love.*

*"We love, because He first loved us."*

*I John 4:19 (NASB)*

The truth of the matter is that none of us could ever love God until He stretched out His hands and died. As a result, we must

---

7 Wuest, K. S. (1997). Wuest's word studies from the Greek New Testament: for the English reader (1 Jn. 4:7). Grand Rapids: Eerdmans.

realize that at the very core of God's being is His desire to show the world how much He loves us. This is the foundation of what it means to be rooted and grounded in love. Living in this revelation, helps us to understand the rest of what scripture says concerning love, that we will be exploring through the remainder of this book.

> *"A man will not be established by wickedness, but **the root of the righteous will not be moved**."*

> *Proverbs 12:3 (NASB)*

Prayer Focus:
Heavenly Father, I pray that you would enable me, through the power of your Spirit that dwells in me, to comprehend your love so that I can come into Your fullness, and experience this manifesting in my life. In Jesus' name, amen.

# CHAPTER 2

# Worth

OVER THE PAST NUMBER OF years God has been speaking to me about our incredible worth. There is something very powerful that happens inside when we come to realize how valuable we are to God. There is also a confidence that comes out of this understanding that makes us secure and immovable through all that life throws at us as Christians. Let me help you begin to see the magnitude of your worth with this simple story.

There were two boys walking down a gravel road, kicking a rock back and forth between them, as they went. As an older gentleman approached the boys, he saw the rock that they were casually kicking, and bent over to pick it up. The man asked if the boys knew what they were kicking around. The boys shrugged their shoulders in response. They boys' eyes got large as saucers when the older man explained that the 'rock' was actually a large, rough-cut diamond, worth thousands of dollars. Because the boys had no idea what they were kicking, they did not see any value in it, and they saw it as nothing more than a meaning- less pebble to be toyed with.

Consider the diamond for a moment... Does it know that it has worth? The truth is that a diamond has no idea its worth, nor is it able to comprehend such things. A diamond can never know it's worth until someone comes and ascribes value to it. Value determines what people are willing to pay, and we know that in our world, diamonds have incredible value.

Considering these thoughts, we should think of our own value in the same way. How does a person know what they are worth? How can we begin to discover our value? What transpires in the core of our being, when we discover what we are worth? Perhaps you, or someone you know, have suffered with a low self-esteem, or negative self-image. I would like to show you love, by helping you see yourself from and entirely different perspective. It is possible for one to go through their entire life, even as a believer in Jesus Christ, feeling insignificant due to an incomplete or inaccurate picture of worth. The million-dollar question is, do you know your worth?

We enter into this world having had our value diminished because of sin. What is the root of the problem, which led to man's lack of esteem? In answer to this, we have to look at man's beginnings. The Bible begins with man's genesis, by explaining the nature and essence of man's creation and the intimacy he once had with God.

> *"Then God said,* **"Let Us make man in Our image,**
> **according to Our like- ness;** *and* **let them rule**
> *over the Osh of the sea and over the birds of the sky and*
> *over the cattle and over all the earth, and over every*
> *creeping thing that creeps on the earth."* **God created**

> **man in His own image, in the image of God He**
> **created him; male and female He created them."**

*Genesis 1:26-27 (NASB)*

In the beginning, the bible says that God made man in His image and His like-ness.

The reason God created man was for the purpose of having an intimate relationship with Him. We can see this illustrated very clearly with Jesus, and how He prayed to the Father before His ascension:

> *"I do not pray for these alone [it is not for their sake*
> *only that I make this request], but also for [all]*
> *those who [will ever] believe and trust in Me through*
> *their message,* **that they all may be one; just**
> **as You, Father, are in Me and I in You,** *that*
> *they also may be one in Us, so that the world may*
> *believe [without any doubt] that You sent Me."*

*John 17:20-21 (NASB)*

Man was the crown of His creation, and the first and only part of His created order that was granted access into the Beloved. God's desire for intimacy with man is clearly reflected in the Psalm of David:

> *"For You formed my inward parts; You wove me in my*
> *mother's womb. I will give thanks to You, for I am*

*fearfully and wonderfully made; Wonderful are Your works, And my soul knows it very well. My frame was not hidden from You, When I was made in secret, And skillfully wrought in the depths of the earth; Your eyes have seen my unformed substance; And in Your book were all written the days that were ordained for me, when as yet there was not one of them."*

Psalm 139:13-16 (NASB) A Psalm of David.

Adam walked with God in the cool of the day in the garden, which reflects this intimacy showing that it was God's intention from the beginning. Why did the simplicity of this continued encounter with God become violated? Because sin entered into the world, man became separated from the only One who could accurately ascribe him his worth.

*"But **your iniquities have made a separation between you and your God,** and **your sins have hidden His face from you so that He does not hear."***

Isaiah 59:2 (NASB)

Without someone to speak our worth to us, we enter into this world in a devalued state. Because God, our creator, is the only one who can truly ascribe our worth, man has been earnestly, yet unsuccessfully trying to find his worth ever since. Consider someone who struggles with addiction... I need a drink... Why?

To help me feel better... Why? I don't feel good about myself. With no ascribed value, we are left without significance and without hope in this world. What we need is to have God the Father come down and breathe His life on us, much like He did with Adam at the time of creation. We need to have Him infuse us with His love, so that we can know our worth and experience what it means to feel approved of and valued. Our entire identity and value is hidden in this declaration:

## "GOD LOVES YOU!"

How does the Father show us what we are worth? Keep in mind that oftentimes, value is determined by what a person is willing to pay for something.

> *"The coveted Holy Grail of baseball cards is the American Tobacco Company's T206 card of Honus Wagner. This card was pulled from circulation after 200 had made it to market because Wagner didn't want to support tobacco use for his young fans. A PSA 8 version (highest surviving grade) of the card traded hands with hockey star Wayne Gretzky and others. The card was discovered to have trimmed edges, which would greatly reduce its value, but that didn't stop Arizona Diamond- backs owner Ken Kendricks to purchase the card in a 2007 auction for $2.8 million."*[8]

---

8  www.therichest.com/luxury/.../the-20-most-expensive-sports-trading-cards-ever-sold/

Most people in their right mind would never spend 2.8 million dollars on a baseball card. However, to illustrate the point in the most ridiculous way, the more we are willing to pay, the more value an item has. God the Father showed us our value by paying the greatest price that was ever paid; Jesus Christ. ***God so loved the world, that He gave… (John 3:16 NASB)***

> *"Just as the Son of Man did not come to be served, but to serve, and **to give His life a ransom** for many."*
>
> *Matthew 20:28 (NASB)*

> *The definition of the word "**ransom**" is "the means or instrument by which release or deliverance is made possible—means of release, ransom".*[9]

> *"For there is one God, and one mediator also between God and men, the man Christ Jesus, **who gave Himself as a ransom for all**, the testimony given at the proper time."*
>
> *1 Timothy 2:5-6 (NASB)*

---

9  Louw, J. P., & Nida, E. A. (1996). Greek-English lexicon of the New Testament: based on semantic domains (electronic ed. of the 2nd edition., Vol. 1, p. 487). New York: United Bible Societies.

> *"Or do you not know that your body is a temple of the*
> *Holy Spirit who is in you, whom you have from God, and*
> *that you are not your own? For* **you have been bought**
> **with a price***: therefore glorify God in your body."*

1 Corinthians 6:19-20 (NASB)

The Bible tells us that we have been bought and paid for by the shed blood of the Son of God. Now ask yourself, 'Who do I belong to?' The Bible also repeatedly assures us that we belong to God. God exchanged His own Son for you! How much does that make you worth?

The Cross of Jesus Christ clearly substantiates your value. Nobody has ever, or could ever pay a greater price than God paid for you. You are acceptable and you are valuable! God saw your worth and paid the ultimate price even while we were still sinners!

> *"But* **God demonstrates His own love toward us,** *in that*
> *while we were yet sinners, Christ died for us." Romans 5:8 (NASB)*

We weren't polished diamonds, but lost, helpless wretched human beings that God loved. When we consider the purchase price paid, the precious blood of Christ, then we have to become convinced of our immense value to God.

When Jesus began His public ministry, what was the first thing that happened? God the Father spoke to Jesus the Son and said:

*"and behold, a voice out of the heavens said, "**This is My beloved Son, in whom I am well-pleased**".*

*Matthew 3:17 (NASB)*

*The word "**beloved**" is defined: "pertaining to one who is the only one of his or her class, but at the same time is particularly loved and cherished—'only, only dear."*[10]

*"**Just as the Father has loved Me, I have also loved you**; abide in My love."*

*John 15:9 (NASB)*

*"The love of the Father toward his only-begotten Son is the highest affection of which we can conceive."*[11]

*"to the praise of the glory of His grace, by which He made us accepted in the Beloved."*

*Ephesians 1:6 (NASB)*

---

10  Louw, J. P., & Nida, E. A. (1996). Greek-English lexicon of the New Testament: based on semantic domains (electronic ed. of the 2nd edition., Vol. 1, p. 590). New York: United Bible Societies.

11  www.sacred-texts.com

There is no way for us to know our value apart from somebody speaking it into our life and validating our son-ship. God assures us that we are His sons; begotten of Him and welcomed into the Beloved, and we are now loved and cherished by Him.

Now that we know our incredible worth, there are a few things I want us to see in light of this precious reality.

With the assurance and confidence of our worth, there are several things that begin to happen in our lives. If we get our value from what God paid through His Son to purchase us, can anyone ever add or take away from what God has done? When we know the value that God has placed on us, there is nothing in this life can add or subtract from it! This includes critical words or lies, curses spoken, and even blessings or compliments that were withheld.

Can the lack of an earthly father add or subtract? Can the loss of a job? Can the lack of affection? The Apostle Paul wrote these very fitting words:

> *"For **I am convinced that neither death, nor life, nor angels, nor principalities, nor things present, nor things to come, nor powers, nor height, nor depth, nor any other created thing, will be able to separate us from the love of God**, which is in Christ Jesus our Lord."*

> *Romans 8:38-39 (NASB)*

Is there anything in this earth that can diminish our value? Absolutely not! My friend, if we could fully realize this, we would be immoveable! One more thing... We cannot have revelation of our value, while at the same time neglect to realize how valuable everyone around us is in God's eyes.

How can we be angry with someone that God loves so much? In light of this, we should exercise the same love, grace and mercy that was shown to us by the one who paid such a high price.

> *"No matter how much the saint experiences of the love of Christ, yet there are oceans of love in the great heart of God that have not been touched by his experience. One is reminded of the words of that saint of old who penned the following lines on the walls of his cell regarding the love of God; "Could we with ink the ocean fill, and were the skies of parchment made; were every stalk on earth a quill, and every man a scribe by trade; to write the love of God above, would drain the ocean dry; nor could the scroll contain the whole, though stretched from sky to sky."[12]*

Prayer Focus:
Father in heaven, I pray that we would never lose sight of our incredible worth. Help us to see the value that you placed on us by giving us Your son on the cross. In Jesus' name, Amen!

12  Wuest, K. S. (1997). Wuest's word studies from the Greek New Testament: for the English reader (Eph. 3:17). Grand Rapids: Eerdmans.

CHAPTER 3
# Fearless

WHEN I THINK BACK ON my childhood, I recall how life was simple, and packed with fun-filled days. I can recall one day in particular, when my childhood friend, David, and I were going to have a sleepover. I don't think my mind was on schoolwork at all that day, as all we could think and talk about were the plans for later that evening. As soon as that final bell rang, we were out the door as quick as our feet would go. That blanket and pillow fort went up even before anyone knew we were in the house. A couple of hours later, we were getting ready to settle in for the night, when out of the blue the telephone rang. David's dad came up the stairs and told me that my dad was on the phone and wanted to talk. Wanting to get the phone call over with, so I could get back to the fort, I skipped down the stairs to the phone. I was surprised by the angry tone on the other end of the line, as my father ordered me to get home. I didn't know exactly what I was in for, but based on the feeling of dread in the pit of my stomach, I knew it wasn't going to be good.

We only lived about four doors down from David's place, but I can tell you that this walk was the longest few minutes of my life. My feet felt like they weighed fifty pounds, as I slowly crept up the steps to my front door. My mind was racing, and I tried to think back to what I could possibly have done to warrant this predicament. As young children often do, I allowed my imagination to get the better of me, as I envisioned the situation to be far worse than it really was. With each passing second, the fear of my father's anger was getting larger and more exaggerated. Trying to soothe my mind, I tried to convince myself that he couldn't really be that upset with me, because after all, who could ever be mad at me? I was a very likable kid...

As I slowly opened the door, my father was standing in the hall waiting for me. With a tone that I was not accustomed to hearing, he asked me to come and sit down. He proceeded to ask me if I had any idea why he had called me to come home. He read my silence to mean that I didn't have any idea, but I deduced that he was about to clue me in, whether I wanted to know the details or not. Earlier that week I had gone into my father's top drawer and pulled out several one hundred dollar bills and was flashing them in front of my friends like I was wealthy. True to childhood nature, one of my friends told his dad what I had done, and word got back to my father. Seems harmless enough, but my father had previously told me that I was forbidden from going into his dresser drawers, and I had knowingly disobeyed him. He told me that I was going to get punished for my disobedience, and he proceeded to give me a good spanking. Thinking back, the spanking wasn't the worst part of the punishment, but the fact that my sleepover was cancelled, was icing on the not so tasty cake.

The part of my story that I want to emphasize for you is the overwhelming fear that I felt, as a young child, going to stand before my father when I knew that he was upset with me. Don't get me wrong, I have a great father, and I can probably count on one hand the times that I received punishment like this. I can't help but suspect that the scenario would have played out differently, had my father simply said that he wanted me to come home to speak with me, without mention of impending punishment. The bible confirms my suspicion of this, when it tells us:

> *"**There is no fear in love**; but perfect love casts out fear, **because fear involves punishment**, and the one who fears is not perfected in love."*
>
> *I John 4:18 (NASB)*

The expectation of punishment is a powerful force for anyone, especially a child. As far back as I can remember, I recall preachers saying things like; "if you look upon God and there is any sin in your life you would be erased from existence". Why would anyone ever want to come before a God that could possibly erase them from existence? God has good reason to act this way toward mankind, due to our sin, but His love covers a multitude of sins, for which we should be eternally grateful.

*"for all have sinned and fall short of the glory of God,"*

*Romans 3:23 (NASB)*

*"For the wages of sin is death, but the free gift of God is eternal life in Christ Jesus our Lord."*

*Romans 6:23 (NASB)*

If we consider ourselves standing before a holy God, in light of these previous passages of Scripture, we have the perfect recipe for fear, which will in turn produce a reluctance to ever come before Him. God is holy and there is no denying this fact, but something had to happen in the hearts of men, that would allow them to approach God without fear. It seems to me that in our efforts to paint a picture of God's holiness, God has been demonized in the eyes of mankind so much that He has become completely unapproachable. How can we reconcile the idea of God being unapproachable with the words of the Apostle Paul who writes:

*"This was in accordance with the eternal purpose which He carried out in Christ Jesus our Lord, in whom **we have boldness and confident access through faith in Him**."*

*Ephesians 3:11-12 (NASB)*

On one hand, God seems to be unapproachable, but on the other the Bible clearly tells us that we should approach Him with confidence. This seems somewhat contradictory. Has God lowered His standards within the context of our New Covenant relationship, that He would allow anyone to approach Him? The truth is God remains the same yesterday today and forever (Hebrews 13:8), so something had to change in order for man to be able to approach Him without fear. Jesus became sin for us, and the wrath of the punishment of sin fell upon Him.

> **"He made Him who knew no sin to be**
> **sin on our behalf,** *so that we might become*
> *the righteousness of God in Him."*

> *2 Corinthians 5:21 (NASB)*

> *"But He was pierced through for our transgressions,*
> *He was crushed for our iniquities; The*
> *chastening for our wellbeing fell upon Him,*
> *and* **by His scourging we are healed."**

> *Isaiah 53:5 (NASB)*

> **"He who believes in the Son has eternal**
> **life;** *but he who does not obey the Son will not*
> *see life, but the wrath of God abides on him."*

> *John 3:36 (NASB)*

If you read over these scriptures quickly you will miss out on some of the most freeing powerful truths. John is saying that when we believe in Jesus, we have already passed into eternal life. This is a past tense action on behalf of God toward those who believe in the Son of God for salvation. It is already done! For those who reject God's gift of salvation, the bible says that the wrath of God still abides on them. They are voluntarily subjecting themselves to come under the hand of the Almighty, for judgment in the last great day of the Lord.

> *"Some of you may not like this, but it's true. Sin isn't a problem with God anymore. It's the church that has made it a major deal. Neither past, present, nor future sins can separate you from God. The only people who will go to hell are those who have spurned and rejected the greatest sacrifice that has ever been made. In heaven, you won't answer for your sin; Jesus already has. You will answer for your acceptance or rejection of Jesus."*[13]

Let me ask you this question: Did Jesus die for the sin of the whole world and receive the punishment due or not? If He didn't then we are all still lost in our sin, and the atonement was faulty at best. According to scripture, Jesus became the propitiation for the sin of the entire world. The Apostle John writes:

> *"and He Himself is the propitiation for our sins; and not for ours only, but also for those of the whole world."*
>
> *I John 2:2 (NASB)*

---

13  www.awmi.net

The battle of sin is finished because of the cross of Calvary. For those who believe, they have become the righteousness of God in Christ. If you accept and fully believe this truth, then you will find that because of the Lord our God, and the atoning sacrificial death of Jesus, you never have to be afraid to stand before God. It was God's good pleasure for this to happen on our behalf.

> *"But **the Lord was pleased To crush Him**,*
> *putting Him to grief; If He would render Himself*
> *as a guilt offering, He will see His offspring,*
> *He will prolong His days, And the good pleasure*
> *of the Lord will prosper in His hand. "*

*Isaiah 53:10 (NASB)*

Even though God has done such a great thing for us, there is still a stumbling block being laid by religious people before the church that causes people to live in fear rather than enjoy their relationship with God with- out fear.

> *"For **you have not received a spirit of slavery***
> ***leading to fear again**, but you have received*
> *a spirit of adoption as sons by which we cry out,*
> *"Abba! Father!" The Spirit Himself testifies with*
> *our spirit that we are children of God,"*

*Romans 8:15-16 (NASB)*

We have been brought into oneness with Christ in God, and within the context of this expression of divine love, fear is eradicated.

> *"Fear cannot co-exist in this love realm. The perfect love union that we are talking about expels fear. Fear holds onto an expectation of crisis and judgment (which brings separation) and interpret it as due punishment (a form of karma). It echoes torment and only registers in someone who does not realize the completeness of their love union (with the Father, Son and Spirit and with one another)." 1 John 4:18* [14]

If we are rooted and grounded in love, we know that our sins have been removed in Christ, and the fear of impending punishment is over for those who believe.

> *"At the cross, Jesus subjects himself to disability, and his resurrected body continues to bear his scars as a sign of God's solidarity with humanity."* [15]

> **"Blessed is the man whose sin the Lord will not take into account."**
>
> *Romans 4:8 (NASB)*

---

14  François Du Toit, I John 4:18 Mirror Bible

15  Thomas E. Reynolds

Prayer Focus:

Dear heavenly Father, I am so grateful that you have saved me, and have removed my sin so I can approach you with confidence. I pray that I would walk in this new confidence, knowing that I have a special place in you. I pray that you would remind me daily of the new life I have and that I have been made a new creature in Christ. In Jesus' name. Amen!

CHAPTER 4
# Giver

YEARS AGO, I WAS ON a mission in Mexico, in a small village, with a team from Canada. We were sharing the Gospel with some local villagers, when I observed a religious ritual taking place in the street. We couldn't help but notice the small group of people crawling on their hands and knees along an uphill, rugged cobblestone pathway. Upon inquiry, we learned that they were attempting to show God how penitent they were, in an effort to somehow attain His favor and blessing. In that moment, I began to question my own piety, as I watched the level of dedication being shown by these people, and yet it made me wonder what kind of God would expect people to subject themselves to such extreme action, simply to gain His approval? Does God grant His approval to man, based on man's merit and self-effort?

Several years later, my family and I were getting ready for church, and for us it was a chaotic morning getting ourselves and our two small children ready. It should be noted, that most of that responsibility was shouldered by my amazing wife, and admittedly, I wasn't holding up my end to help, in the process. As a result we had some words and she won the argument, hands down. We made our way to church that morning, and I conducted my pastoral duties, as usual. After I preached the word of God, I felt led to have an altar call to pray for the needs of our congregants.

As the people were coming up to the altar, I was reminded about the argument with Tracy before church, and I left the altar area to go and repent, as I was conditioned to do, so that God would be able to use me to minister to the people. God spoke to my heart very clearly, and said that He and I could later talk about what happened before church. He assured me that He does not use me because I have it all together, and then released me to go and minister to the people. In all honesty, this left me somewhat confused, because God's response went against my performance mentality.

That morning God brought me face to face with a structure of unbelief that I had in my heart. In that moment, my lack of understanding paralyzed me from being effective. I did not see my life from a new creation perspective, as one who had been changed because of the cross. Based on my understanding of repentance, every time I sinned, I had to somehow make things right to regain my proper standing before God, in order to be able to do ministry. I was living like many in the church, with a performance mentality, always trying to be good enough to serve God, trusting in my flesh, rather than from a position of rest in the finished work of Christ. Guy Caley writes:

> *"When washing a child's hair you tell the child to put their head back and they won't get shampoo in their eyes. Their natural reaction is to put their head forward and rub their eyes, every time the water starts to flow."*[16]

When we trust in the one who is doing the work, we won't get shampoo in our eyes. When we try to take control and make things happen, we get shampoo in our eyes every time.

The book of Galatians lays this out powerfully, so if we are going to see the truth, we have to begin there.

> *"You foolish Galatians, who has bewitched you, before whose eyes Jesus Christ was publicly portrayed as crucified? This is the only thing I want to find out from you:* **did you receive the Spirit by the works of the Law, or by hearing with faith?** *Are you so foolish?* **Having begun by the Spirit, are you now being perfected by the flesh?** *Did you suffer so many things in vain—if indeed it was in vain?* **So then, does He who provides you with the Spirit and works miracles among you, do it by the works of the Law, or by hearing with faith?"** *"Even so Abraham believed God, and it was reckoned to him as righteousness. Therefore, be sure that it is those who are of faith who are sons of Abraham. The Scripture, foreseeing that God would justify the Gentiles by faith, preached the gospel beforehand to Abraham, saying, "All*

---

16  www.sermoncentral.com

*the nations will be blessed in you." So then those who*
*are of faith are blessed with Abraham, the believer."*

*Galatians 3:1-9 (NASB)*

In the passage of Galatians, Paul proposes three essential questions to the believers: Did you receive the Spirit by the works of the law, or by hearing with faith? Having begun by the Spirit, are you now being perfected by the flesh? Does He who provides you with the Spirit and works miracles among you, do it by the works of the law, or by hearing with faith?

In addressing the first of Paul's questions, we have to ask; How do we receive the Holy Spirit?

*The word "***receive***" can be defined as:*

*"***to receive or accept an object or benefit for which the initiative rests with the giver***, but the focus of atten-tion in the transfer is upon the receiver—'to receive, receiv-ing, to accept."* [17]

Again, a clear example of this can be seen in one of the most quoted verses in the bible: *"For **God so loved** the world **that He gave**..." John 3:16a (NASB)*

---

17 Louw, J. P., & Nida, E. A. (1996). Greek-English lexicon of the New Testament: based on semantic domains (electronic ed. of the 2nd edition., Vol. 1, p. 571). New York: United Bible Societies.

In this powerful verse, we see that God has always been the initiator of our salvation and our subsequent relationship with Him. The following scriptures indicate that God is the initiator in everything concerning us, and we receive this simply by faith in Jesus Christ.

> *"For **by grace you have been saved through faith**; and that not of yourselves, **it is the gift of God; not as a result of works**, so that no one may boast."*

> *Ephesians 2:8-9 (NASB)*

> *"**But if it is by grace, it is no longer on the basis of works, otherwise grace is no longer grace**."*

> *Romans 11:6 (NASB)*

It is evident from these passages that our receiving the deposit of God's spirit in our lives rests completely with God. God begins a work in us, and He completes it.

> *"**Fixing our eyes on Jesus, the author and perfecter of faith**, who for the joy set before Him endured the cross, despising the shame, and has sat down at the right hand of the throne of God."*

> *Hebrews 12:2 (NASB)*

The second of Paul's questions must be answered because if we are to continue in the faith that was begun in the Spirit, then we cannot now proceed by any other means, which includes any efforts made in the flesh.

> *"Are you so foolish? Having begun by the Spirit,*
> *are you now being perfected by the flesh?"*

> *Galatians 3:3 (NASB)*

Paul's question in Galatians 3:3 begs an answer: How are we perfected? The author of the book of Hebrews does not identify himself, but he writes:

> *"For by one offering* **He has perfected for**
> **all time those who are sanctified**.*"*

> *Hebrews 10:14 (NASB)*

The truth is that we were perfected forever by the perfect sacrifice of the Son of God the moment we trusted Him for salvation. This does not mean that we are not to grow and come into maturity, or that we can continue in sin, but that our spirit man has been made perfect. There is a progressive work of the spirit of God where we are being changed from glory to glory. According to Paul's second letter to the Corinthian church, this change happens when we behold Him, and He does the work in us.

*"but whenever a person turns to the Lord, the
veil is taken away. Now the Lord is the Spirit,
and where the Spirit of the Lord is, there is
liberty. **But we all, with unveiled face,
beholding as in a mirror the glory of the
Lord, are being transformed into the same
image from glory to glory**, just
as from the Lord, the Spirit."*

*II Corinthians 3:16-18 (NASB)*

The third answer to Paul's questions gives us further assurance
that we know that the work and power of the Spirit is not given
to us by works of flesh.

*"Did you suffer so many things in vain—if
indeed it was in vain? So then, does He who
provides you with the Spirit and works
miracles among you, do it by the works of
the Law, or by hearing with faith?"*

*Galatians 3:4-5 (NASB)*

*"**It is the Spirit who gives life; the flesh
profits nothing**; the words that I have
spoken to you are spirit and are life."*

*John 6:63 (NASB)*

Paul is drawing the people back to the simplicity of the way they got saved and how they should continue in it, and that is in "hearing by faith."

This not only applies to Salvation, but also to the work that we do for the Lord while we are here on this earth. The answer to all three of Paul's questions is the end of any performance or striving in the flesh for every believer, and we simply need to continually believe in the one whom God sent for us.

> *"Therefore they said to Him, "What shall we do, so that we may work the works of God?" Jesus answered and said to them, "**This is the work of God, that you believe in Him whom He has sent**."*

*John 6:28-29 (NASB)*

Thinking back to the issue of my structure of unbelief that God revealed to me that Sunday morning, I came to the conclusion that I had been trusting in the works of my own flesh rather than believing in the finished work of Jesus Christ. My friend, this is a powerful truth that we all must come to understand. God wants us to simply trust the Giver, that through His son, He has completely made a way for us to do all things.

> *"I can do all things **through Him who strengthens me**."*

*Philippians 4:13 (NASB)*

Our right standing before God never changes, because we did not produce it through our own self effort, and we do not continue to make it effective through our works. We were made righteous because of His righteousness, and we continue to be righteous because of His righteousness.

> *"He made Him who knew no sin to be sin on our behalf, so that we might become the righteousness of God in Him."*
>
> *2 Corinthians 5:21 (NASB)*

When I felt that God could not use me to minister at the alter that Sunday morning, before I prayed, shows that I didn't understand the completeness of what Jesus had done. I had the wrong perspective.

The reality is, that I never ceased to be in right standing, even after having an argument with my wife.

Thinking again, of the word **"receive"**, it is crucial that we remember that, **"the initiative rests with the giver"**. You can't call yourself a son of Abraham, or a child of faith, because you keep the Law, but because you are a person of faith in Jesus Christ alone! You will never be an effective minister because you do everything right, but only because you put your trust in the one who did do everything right.

Another important element of my misunderstanding that much of the church can identify with is that my ministry was dependent upon me earning God's approval and I was failing to see that I already had it because of the finished work of Christ.

The secret to knowing that we have God's approval begins with these simple words penned by the Apostle John:

> *"For God so loved the world, that He gave His*
> *only begotten Son, that* ***whoever believes in***
> ***Him*** *shall not perish, but have eternal life."*

*John 3:16 (NASB)*

Right believing gives us access to everything God has for us all the time. To be rooted and grounded in the love of God, we must understand and believe this essential truth. The reason God gives anything to the world is simply because of His love. We need to see that John 3:16 cannot be understood apart from that absolute truth which says that God that is love.

> *"The one who does not love does not*
> *know God, for* ***God is love.****"*

*1 John 4:8 (NASB)*

It is not even possible to say that you know God apart from His love, because you could never separate Him from this absolute truth. Our response to a God whose very nature is demonstrated as loving should naturally be to manifest itself in love.

> ***"We love, because He first loved us."***

*I John 4:19 (NASB)*

The truth of the matter is that none of us ever loved God until He stretched out His hands and died. As a result, we can see that the first thing we must realize is that at the very core of God's being is the desire to show the world how much He loves us. God wants to bless you more than you want to be blessed! Will you chose to believe this simple truth today?

Prayer Focus:
Dear heavenly Father, I recognize that you are love, and that you love me deeply. I know that the only reason why I love you is because you showed a tremendous love for me first. In Jesus' name, amen.

CHAPTER 5
# Provide

YEARS AGO, WHEN OUR CHILDREN were toddlers things were very tight for us financially, and we were swimming in a river of debt. It was Thanksgiving Sunday, and we were down to just a few cans of food in the cupboards. On our way to church, Tracy leaned over and sighed as she expressed her desire for a ham for Thanksgiving dinner that day. I pulled the car over, took her hand and we prayed together for God to somehow provide, and then continued on our way to church. I'll be honest, it was somewhat discouraging for us to hear the different conversations of the family plans and big dinners that everyone else seemed to be planning for the Thanksgiving weekend. We arrived home after church, and to our surprise, there were fourteen (yes, we counted) bags of groceries on our table, including the biggest ham we had ever seen. Unbeknownst to us, God had spoken to a woman in our church that morning, at the same time we were praying, about our need. The fact that God would speak to her on our behalf, demonstrates that He was listening, and that He loved us.

In 2010, I was in Ukraine working with an organization called, 'Christ is the Answer', preaching and teaching in several churches. One evening, as I was entering one of the churches, I felt that God was leading me to bless the pastor financially, and so I reached into my pocket and pulled out some money and handed it to him, reminding him of how much God loved him.

What I didn't realize at that moment, was that I had given him everything I had, and I didn't have access to any more funds, with two full weeks of ministry remaining. Truthfully, my heart plummeted, but I reminded myself that God knew, even before I had done it, that I would have need. I gave this to the Lord in prayer and left it in His hands.

> *"Prayer is an acknowledgment that our need*
> *of God's help is not partial but total."*[18]

> **"Be anxious for nothing, but in everything by**
> **prayer and supplication with thanksgiving**
> **let your requests be made known to God."**

> *Philippians 4:6 (NASB)*

Just prior to the service, a man came up to me and handed me some money. Later on in the service, the church took up an offering for me, and I ended up with far more than what I

---

18 Alistair Begg, Made For His Pleasure: Ten Benchmarks of a Vital Faith

started the mission with. Once again, God demonstrated His love and faithfulness to me, in a greater measure than I even envisioned.

Fast forward to one year later, and I was back at that same church in Ukraine. To my surprise, Pastor Vladimir, who has since gone home to be with the Lord, had been taking up regular offerings to fly me back there to minister to his congregation.

He handed me an envelope with offering that the church had collected, and the moment it touched my hand, I felt that Lord tell me that I was supposed to give it away. I chuckled a little, on the inside, thinking that God must be kidding. After all, I was the guy who needed the money. There were two friends that had been praying about leaving Ukraine, and going to Venezuela to pioneer a new ministry. I felt God's leading to give the envelope of money to them.

Later that evening, they came back to me with a tearful expression and asked me if I knew how much money I had given them. The truth is that I hadn't even opened the envelope because from the moment God spoke to me it wasn't mine to open. When they told me that there was a thousand dollars in the envelope, I thought to myself how much I could have used it, and I chuckled again.

When I returned home from Canada, God spoke to a wonderful friend who approached me while I was enjoying a coffee in Tim Horton's and handed me an envelope with four times the amount I had given to the couple in Ukraine. This was enough for both Tracy and I to fly there the next year. There is an old Hymn that I love, and the words express some of the feelings that I have when I recount these stories of God's faithfulness.

> *"'Tis so sweet to trust in Jesus, Just to take Him at His word;*
> *Just to rest upon His promise; Just to know, Thus saith the Lord.*
> *Jesus, Jesus, how I trust Him, How I've proved Him o'er*
> *and o'er, Jesus, Jesus, Precious Jesus! O for grace to trust Him*
> *more."* [19]

The Apostle Matthew wrote:

> *"For this reason I say to you, do not be worried about your life, as to what you will eat or what you will drink; nor for your body, as to what you will put on. Is not life more than food, and the body more than clothing? Look at the birds of the air, that they do not sow, nor reap nor gather into barns, and yet your heavenly Father feeds them.* **Are you not worth much more than they?** *And who of you by being worried can add a single hour to his life? And why are you worried about clothing? Observe how the lilies of the field grow; they do not toil nor do they spin, yet I say to you that not even Solomon in all his glory clothed himself like one of these. But if God so clothes the grass of the field, which is alive today and tomorrow is thrown into the furnace,* **will He not much more clothe you?"**

> *Matthew 6:25-34 (NASB)*

---

19  www.hymnal.net

When we are rooted and grounded in love, we know and understand that because we are of such great value to God, which we discovered in chapter 2, we can trust that He will always provide for us. The words **"how much more"**, shows the heart of the Father for His children. God is a 'much more' kind of Father, who loves to give good gifts to His children. We have to see ourselves as being valuable and loved, so that we can receive God's heart for us, and the blessings that will follow.

> *"So I say to you, ask, and it will be given to you; seek,*
> *and you will find; knock, and it will be opened to*
> *you. For everyone who asks, receives; and he who*
> *seeks, finds; and to him who knocks, it will be opened.*
> *Now suppose one of you fathers is asked by his son*
> *for a fish; he will not give him a snake instead of*
> *a fish, will he? Or if he is asked for an egg, he will*
> *not give him a scorpion, will he? If you then, being*
> *evil, know how to give good gifts to your children,*
> ***how much more will your heavenly Father***
> ***give*** *the Holy Spirit to those who ask Him?"*

*Luke 11:9-13 (NASB)*

In the midst of writing this chapter, I happened to be speaking with my parents about this very subject, and we weren't very long into the conversation, when my mom came to the realization that she could be asking and trusting God for more.

*"...You say to God, "I have never seen you provide for me." God says to you, "You have never trusted Me."* [20]

In order to see God provide, we need to be people who know how to ask. This is so true for the entire body of Christ. God wants us to have far more than we ever think to ask Him for.

> *"Now to Him **who is able to do far more abundantly beyond all that we ask or think**, according to the power that works within us,"*
>
> *Ephesians 3:20 (NASB)*

> *"You lust and do not have; so you commit murder. You are envious and cannot obtain; so you fight and quarrel. **You do not have because you do not ask**."*
>
> *James 4:2 (NASB)*

We need to begin to be courageous in the way we ask God for things, knowing that He delights in us, and loves to give good gifts to His children. Asking of God takes trust and speaks to our dependence upon Him. God wants us to look to Him, with expectation, for all things. Will you make the decision today,

---

20 Corallie Buchanan, Watch Out! Godly Women on the Loose

in the same way that you trusted Him for salvation to trust Him that He will provide all your needs?

> *"And my **God will supply all your needs***
> *according to His riches in glory in Christ Jesus."*

> Philippians 4:19 (NASB)

> *"The best way to handle life, is to put your life in God's hands."*[21]

Prayer Focus:
Dear heavenly Father, I pray that you would help me to remember that you are always ready to hear my prayers, and that you delight in giving me the desires of my heart. Help me never to feel that my asking is in any way, unimportant to you. Help me to look to you more, so I can see you moving in my life, in a greater way. In Jesus' name, Amen!

---

21  Anthony Liccione

CHAPTER 6

# Knowing

ONE OF THE GREATEST PURSUITS of my life has been to have God encounters where I can hear His voice and have Him speak to me in such a way as to change lives; my own included. Let me share a few of them with you, and it is my heart to inspire your faith and encourage you into the deeper things of the Spirit.

*"and let us consider how to stimulate one
another to love and good deeds,"*

*Hebrews 10:24 (NASB)*

One day I was sitting alone in Tim Horton's, one of our most popular coffee hotspots, enjoying a few minutes of down time, enjoying my cup of coffee. Unexpectedly, I heard the Lord speak to my spirit, "Tell the guy that's coming in the door that he needs to turn his heart back to me". Upon hearing these words from the Lord for the man, I stood up and proceeded toward the door and gave him the message. Immediately, the man's countenance changed and his eyes welled up with tears. He explained to me that the night before, he was listening to a song on the radio about turning your heart back to the Lord. The man was a backslidden Christian who really needed to know that God cared and hadn't forgotten about him.

Last year we were doing some preaching in the Philippines, and God gave me a word of knowledge in picture form, showing me a cancerous tumor being cut away, as well as a girl playing a violin. Because I had no knowledge of the group to which I was ministering, I had no idea who played the violin or who had the cancer. Being obedient, I simply asked the congregation if there was a violin player in the assembly and also asked the person with the tumor to come forward. There was a young girl and an elderly woman who slowly walked forward when I gave the call. The elderly woman had a tumor on her neck. What I found out, after the fact, was that there had been two people who were suffering from cancer, but using the girl who played the violin, God was showing the one He was going to heal. The girl who played the violin was the granddaughter of the elderly woman with the tumor! We prayed for the cancer to die, and a few weeks later we received word from the Philippines that the lady was healed. Praise the Lord!

A few years ago my son, Graham, and I went out with a team to do some street evangelism. Before going out, I asked the Lord if there were any specific things we could do, or if there were things I could know before going out, that would help us. God proceeded to give me a series of pictures that I wrote down on a piece of paper and put in my pocket. On the paper, I wrote bicycles, a woman with long dark hair, the number 21 and I saw a hand touch a pain in the lower right side of the back. A few hours later my son and I were walking in the park, and I saw some bicycles, and I heard a woman complain about a pain in her back. I turned and saw that she had long dark hair.

I approached her and asked her age and she said that she was twenty-one years old. I reached inside my pocket and pulled out the piece of paper with what God told me. I then began to tell her of how I had been in prayer earlier that evening, and God showed me these things, because He wanted to heal her. I called out to everyone that was around us to come, and my son and I prayed for her. We proceeded to preach the Gospel to everyone there, as they witnessed her being touched by the Lord Jesus.

You may be wondering how these things can happen, and I can only say, that it's by the grace and power of Almighty God. My purpose in sharing these accounts with you is to ignite your faith, and open up your realization to the potential of what God can do in and through your life. The Apostle Paul writes:

> *"and my message and my preaching were not in persuasive words of wisdom, but in demonstration of the Spirit and of power, so that your faith would not rest on the wisdom of men, but on the power of God."*

> *I Corinthians 2:4-5 (NASB)*

Our desire, as God's people, should lean toward walking in the Spirit and demonstrating His power, so that the world knows that what we are doing is from God and not from ourselves.

These encounters can be happening in every believer's life on a regular basis. You may be wondering what you have to do, in order for God to use you in these ways. In the remaining part of this chapter, I am going to teach you some keys to develop your ability to hear and see what the Father is doing, so that you can manifest His goodness in every place.

The first thing we need to understand is that God wants to make Himself known to the world. He is not playing a game of cosmic hide and seek, trying to avoid mankind.

> ""For **the earth will be filled with the knowledge of the glory of the Lord**, *as the waters cover the sea."*

*Habakkuk 2:14 (NASB)*

> *"God, after He spoke long ago to the fathers in the prophets in many portions and in many ways, in these last days has spoken to us in His Son, whom He appointed heir of all things, through whom also He made the world. And He is the radiance of His glory and the exact representation of His nature, and upholds all things by the word of His power. When He had made purification of sins, He sat down at the right hand of the Majesty on high,"*

*Hebrews 1:1-3 (NASB)*

Jesus is the patterned Son, and it is because of Him that God can speak to us in these last days. Jesus came to reveal what a son looks like, how we are to operate and communicate with God the Father.

Several years ago now I had a night that I will never forget. I had gone to bed and was fast asleep when all of a sudden the first of seven blasts of wind shook my house. With each blast of wind, I could feel the presence of God stirring me. When the last blast of wind came, so did the word of the Lord. I sat up in my bed and the Lord gave me Isaiah 11:1-3.

> *"Then a shoot will spring from the stem of Jesse, and*
> *a branch from his roots will bear fruit. The Spirit of*
> *the Lord will rest on Him, the spirit of wisdom and*
> *understanding, the spirit of counsel and strength,*
> *the spirit of knowledge and the fear of the Lord.*
> *And He will delight in the fear of the Lord, and*
> ***He will not judge by what His eyes see, nor***
> ***make a decision by what His ears hear;"***

> *Isaiah 11:1-3 (NASB)*

The portion of the verse that stood out to my spirit was; **"He will not judge by what His eyes see, nor make a decision by what His ears hear."** For several days I pondered these things, and then I saw the secret for all of us who are called as sons to be able to hear and see God in the same way.

> *"Therefore Jesus answered and was saying to*
> *them, "Truly, truly, I say to you, the Son can do*
> *nothing of Himself, unless it is something He sees*

> the Father doing; for whatever the Father does,
> these things the Son also does in like manner.
>
> For **the Father loves the Son, and shows**
> **Him all things that He Himself is doing;**
> and the Father will show Him greater works
> than these, so that you will marvel."
>
> John 5:19-20 (NASB)

If we are rooted and grounded in love, we will understand that because we are the sons of God, the words **"the father loves the son, and shows Him all things that He Himself is doing"** will ring true for us. This truth is rooted in John 3:16; "God so loved the world that He gave." God gives to humanity simply because it is His divine nature, and it is the longing of His heart to express Himself toward us with love. Our ability to know things from God comes because we have been given His Spirit, and we have this because of His divine love that is constantly being shown to us. God wants to reveal Himself, and make what He knows, known to us and to the world. He is waiting for His people to move toward Him in the Spirit, and receive all He has. The Apostle Paul explains this in great detail in his letter to the Corinthian church.

> "Yet we do speak wisdom among those who are mature;
> a wisdom, how- ever, not of this age nor of the rulers
> of this age, who are passing away; but we speak God's
> wisdom in a mystery, the hidden wisdom which God

*predestined before the ages to our glory; the wisdom which none of the rulers of this age has understood; for if they had understood it they would not have crucified the Lord of glory; but just as it is written,* **"Things which eye has not seen and ear has not heard, and which have not entered the heart of man,** *all that God has prepared for those who love Him." For* **to us God revealed them through the Spirit;** *for* **the Spirit searches all things, even the depths of God.** *For who among men knows the thoughts of a man except the spirit of the man which is in him? Even so* **the thoughts of God no one knows except the Spirit of God.** *Now* **we have received, not the spirit of the world, but the Spirit who is from God, so that we may know the things freely given to us by God,** *which things we also speak, not in words taught by human wisdom, but in those taught by the Spirit, combining spiritual thoughts with spiritual words.*

*But a natural man does not accept the things of the Spirit of God, for they are foolishness to him; and he cannot understand them, because they are spiritually appraised. But he who is spiritual appraises all things, yet he himself is appraised by no one. For who has known the mind of the Lord, that he will instruct Him? But we have the mind of Christ."*

*I Corinthians 2:6-16 (NASB)*

There is so much revelation in this passage of scripture, and I want to break it down for us, because hidden in these words is the template for hearing and seeing the deep things that God so longs to speak to us.

Until the time of Jesus, the human senses had never comprehended the depths of what God had prepared for those who love Him. However, it says to us these things were being revealed by God through the Spirit. The Spirit has the ability to search the deep things of God that nobody has ever seen, heard or understood. They were mysteries that were hidden, but God chose to make them known.

How can we understand these mysteries? The mysteries are the thoughts of God that nobody knows except the Spirit of God, which is what we have according to this passage. Think about this for a moment. We have the Spirit of God that searches the deep things of God enabling us to see and hear the mysteries of God that only He knows. We have the Spirit of God so that we can know the things freely given to us by God. What this means, is that the things our eye has not seen, we can now see! This means that the things the ear has never heard, we can now hear!

There is another secret that Paul is revealing here in this passage, and it has to do with the tools we have been given, to decipher the spiritual information.

> *"Now **we have received**, not the spirit of the world,*
> *but **the Spirit who is from God, so that we may**
> **know the things freely given to us by God**,*

> *which things we also speak, not in words taught by*
> *human wisdom, but in those taught by the Spirit,*
> *combining spiritual thoughts with spiritual words."*

*I Corinthians 2:12-13 (NASB)*

The moment that we received the baptism in the Holy Spirit, and spoke in tongues, we began to speak words taught by the Spirit, and were now able to combine spiritual thoughts with spiritual words. Praying in tongues reveals mysteries, as it goes into the deep things of God like a bucket being lowered into a well to draw water.

> *"For **one who speaks in a tongue** does not*
> *speak to men but to God; for no one understands,*
> ***but in his spirit he speaks mysteries**."*

*I Corinthians 14:2 (NASB)*

When we pray in the Spirit, we are speaking mysteries. These are the mysteries of God, which eye has not seen, and ear has not heard. When we speak these mysteries we are given spiritual thoughts, which are the words, pictures and understandings of God that are deciphered in our imagination. God wants us to know all things that He has freely given to us, and this is the process. We must pray in the Spirit without ceasing!

The devil would like to blind us to the idea of praying in the Spirit, and hinder us when we do, because we are dangerous to the kingdom of darkness when we know and understand spiritual things. Why does God speak to us?

> *"For **the Father loves the Son, and shows Him all things that He Himself is doing;**"*

*John 5:20 (NASB)*

Why does God show the Son what He is doing? The answer is simple; because the Father loves the loves the Son. Are you starting to see a pattern emerging?

> *"**Because you are sons, God has sent forth the Spirit of His Son into our hearts, crying, "Abba! Father!"**"*

*Galatians 4:6 (NASB)*

> *"**See how great a love the Father has bestowed on us, that we would be called children of God; and such we are.**"*

*I John 3:1 (NASB)*

*A friend of mine, Marc Brisebois, was telling me recently, about a famous, well known prophetic man who was sitting in a restaurant one day. As the man of God sat there, his heart was flooded with words of knowledge for people spread throughout the busy restaurant. The man asked God, for what purpose He had shared all these words with him, considering the fact that he couldn't do anything about it. He heard God respond, "because you are my friend".* [22]

You are more than a mere friend, you are His son, and He loves you, and wants to reveal to you the depths of what He contains in His heart! Do you believe this? Will you begin to pray in the Spirit and allow Him to reveal these mysteries to you?

> *"Teach us to know that we cannot know, for the things*
> *of God knoweth no man, but the Spirit of God. Let*
> *faith support us where reason fails, and we shall think*
> *because we believe, not in order that we may believe."* [23]

> *"'Call to Me and I will answer you, and I will tell you*
> *great and mighty things, which you do not know.'"*

*Jeremiah 33:3 (NASB)*

Prayer Focus:
Dear heavenly Father, help me to know that the world needs to see your power in my life so that they know I am from you.

---

22  Paul Cain

23  A.W. Tozer, The Knowledge of the Holy

Help me to see that you have given me the ability to see and hear the hidden mysteries of your heart. Help me to see that the reason you speak to me is because of your deep love for me as your child. In Jesus' name, amen!

# CHAPTER 7

# Near

EARLY THIS PAST SPRING, I was having a very difficult time with nausea and weakness, having recently had surgery. One afternoon as I was lying on my bed and aimlessly scrolling through Facebook, a live video came on with Reinhard Bonnke, the German Evangelist, asking if any of his listeners were feeling weak. God began to speak to me in my moment of weakness, and I would like to share some of these thoughts with you.

The word of the Lord that came to me when I was feeling weak was "I am with you…" I just wept when I heard the Lord impress this truth on my heart. In that moment, in the quietness of my bedroom, I began to speak His name over and over. With each time I spoke the name of Jesus, His presence began to rise on the inside of me, and His strengthening virtue came.

There is a confidence that comes when we realize that we are not alone. Quite often I hear Christians praying and asking God to come and be with them. In light of the realization that God is always near, it seems a little misguided for us to ask God to come be with us. Consider what the bible says about God being present with us:

> *"Behold, the virgin shall be with child and shall*
> *bear a Son, and they shall call His name Immanuel,"*
> *which translated means, "**God with us.**"*

*Matthew 1:23 (NASB)*

Written here, as plain as day, is one of the names of Jesus, which is translated '**God with us**'. As Jesus was about to leave His disciples to join the Father at His right hand, He gave commands to them and reminded them that He would always be with them.

> *"teaching them to observe all that I commanded you; and*
> *lo, **I am with you always**, even to the end of the age."*

*Matthew 28:20 (NASB)*

> *"So then, when the Lord Jesus had spoken to them,*
> *He was received up into heaven and sat down at the*
> *right hand of God. And they went out and preached*
> *everywhere, while **the Lord worked with them**,*
> *and confirmed the word by the signs that followed."*

*Mark 16:19-20 (NASB)*

Consider the implication of the words Mark uses in this passage. "The Lord worked with them," demonstrates to me that He was present when the works were being manifested by the disciples. I have come to understand that when I stretch forth my hand to pray for the sick, His hand is outstretched as well.

Consider also, the life of Joshua, as he was to succeed Moses in taking the people of Israel into the Promised Land. Joshua had big shoes to fill, and had always leaned on Moses for direction and leadership. Now Joshua was the man in charge, and he was going at it alone without Moses. Before Joshua began his leadership, God gave him a very powerful affirmation:

> *"Have I not commanded you? Be strong and courageous!*
> *Do not tremble or be dismayed, for **the Lord***
> ***your God is with you wherever you go**."*

*Joshua 1:9 (NASB)*

This is the very same affirmation that He gives to all of us who are His sons and daughters. To remind you of a scripture I mentioned earlier, Jesus said: **"I am with you always, even to the end of the age"**. The end of the church age has not yet happened, and this tells me that the promise of God is still very much active. The prophet Isaiah affirms the very same words yet again:

> *"'Do not fear, for **I am with you**; do not*
> *anxiously look about you, for I am your God. I*
> *will strengthen you, surely I will help you, surely I*
> *will uphold you with My righteous right hand."*

*Isaiah 41:10 (NASB)*

As a teenager, my grandmother spoke these words of Jesus to me. When at the age of twenty, I overdosed on drugs by accident, I clearly recall hearing those words in my mind, as I struggled to come around. God was reminding me that He was with me, and it gave me courage to call out to Him.

> *"Be strong and courageous, do not be afraid or tremble*
> *at them, for the Lord your **God is the one who goes***
> ***with you. He will not fail you or forsake you**."*
>
> *Deuteronomy 31:6 (NASB)*

When you read these words **"he will never leave you or forsake you,"** you can't escape the truth of His continual presence. Going back to the first few months after my salvation experience, I had a radical encounter with God. I was reading the book of Jeremiah, and I had a vision from the Lord, where He showed me a picture of myself speaking to many dark faces. When I awoke from the vision, I prayed, knowing that God had called me to the ministry, despite the fact that I was horrified at the though of speaking in public. I can remember saying these words to the Lord in my prayer; "Lord, if you want me to minister for you, I will, but the first time I go to speak, would you come and sit on my head like a helmet so I know that you are with me?" It was a couple of years later when I was asked to preach my first sermon, and when I opened my mouth to speak the first word, I reassuringly felt the presence of God, as though He were literally on my head.

Part of the call that God has placed on my life has included going to various nations.

This meant that I had to confront my fear of high places, and get on airplanes, to fly around the world. When I first began flying, I would constantly remind myself that God was with me, and that even if the unthinkable happened, I would be present with the Lord. Knowing that God is near removes fear and anxiety. When you are deeply rooted in the love of God, you will recognize that God is always with you. The love of God affirms His presence with us.

How does the world know that God is with us? The world knows that God is with us, because of the measure of the Spirit we walk in. Jesus was approached by a Pharisee names Nicodemus in the middle of the night:

> *"Now there was a man of the Pharisees, named Nicodemus, a ruler of the Jews; this man came to Jesus by night and said to Him, "Rabbi, **we know that You have come from God as a teacher; for no one can do these signs that You do unless God is with him**."*

*John 3:1-2 (NASB)*

The world will know that God is with you as you demonstrate His power. One of my prayers, before I ever begin to speak in any of my meetings, is that God would show the people that He is with me, by manifesting His power through my life, and through my words. The Apostle Paul writes:

> *"I was with you in weakness and in fear and in much trembling, and my message and my preaching were not in*

*persuasive words of wisdom, but in demonstration of the*
*Spirit and of power,* **so that your faith would not rest**
**on the wisdom of men, but on the power of God**.*"*

*I Corinthians 2:3-5 (NASB)*

I know that there will be times in your life when you are feeling weak, but I want to let you know that it is in those times, He is ready to say; "here I am!"

**"The Lord is near to all who call upon**
**Him**, *to all who call upon Him in truth."*

*Psalm 145:18 (NASB)*

*"We need never shout across the spaces to an absent God. He is nearer than our own soul, closer than our most secret thoughts"*[24]

Prayer Focus:
Dear heavenly Father, I pray that you would help me realize that You are always with me. Remind me of this when I am struggling to know that you are there. In Jesus' name. Amen!

---

24  A.W. Tozer The Pursuit of God

CHAPTER 8
# Goodness

WHEN VISITING AN ANIMAL SHELTER, one gets to see all kinds of animals, both healthy and unhealthy. It's not difficult to distinguish which potential adoptees have come from an abusive situation. Rather than appearing sad or lonely, the abused animals are usually withdrawn, and often quite aggressive when approached by a stranger. Despite one's kindest intention, these animals have an instinct to protect themselves. When they anticipate a threat, then immediately go into defense mode. You can't blame the animal for trying to get out of the way if they think that they are going to be beaten. Again, you may have the best of intentions toward the animal, and you may also be the most tenderhearted person that would never hurt a dog, but they don't know that. The wounded animal sees you through the lens of their wounded heart; much like people tend to do when they've been wounded by another person.

A new owner of a formerly abused animal would have to work hard and demonstrate a tremendous amount of patience and love, in order to gain their trust. God wants us to know that He has our best intentions in mind all of the time, and He wants us to trust Him. If we are rooted and grounded in love we will know this in a real way.

One of the most difficult and time-consuming elements of any relationship is establishing trust. A critical aspect of building this foundation of trust is the requirement for both parties to let their guard down, and voluntarily make themselves vulnerable. Difficult situations in life, prior damaging relationships, or other life disappointments, often make us wary of completely trusting another person with our most inner selves. Will they hurt me? Will they take advantage of me? Can I really be convinced that they have my best intentions in mind? The truth is, we will all face moments of hurt from the people that we allow to truly know us, but the steps we take immediately following the hurt, are absolutely critical. Generally speaking, our first inclination is oftentimes just like that of the abused animal; self defense mode.

A telltale sign that you are lacking in the area of trust is evidenced by your immediate reaction to criticism, accusation, slander, or other words you deem as being in some way hurtful. Your reaction demonstrates whether you are trusting God or self-preserving. How much do you trust God to be your defender, provider, and comforter? Do you trust that God will work for your absolute best if you don't defend yourself? A friend of mine, Chris Scarinzi, recently shared these words with me:

> *"When you sit down, God stands up, and when you stand up
> God sits down."*[25]

Whether you are in need of provision, protection, or simply God's hand to move on your behalf, this statement applies. When you sit down, or purpose to not react in self-defense, you are letting God stand up and fight for you. As human beings, our pride tends to get in the way, which only serves to prolong our struggle, rather than humble ourselves and ask our God for help.

Much like a rabbit that gets it's neck caught in a snare; the more it struggles to free itself, the tighter the snare becomes. Our response, when challenged, can be used as a measuring stick to evaluate how deeply rooted and grounded we are in the love of God.

> *"And we know that God causes all things to work
> together for good to those who love God, to those
> who are called according to His purpose."*
>
> *Romans 8:28 (NASB)*

The Mirror Bible translates this verse the following way:

> *"Meanwhile we know that the love of God causes everything to
> mutually contribute to our advantage..."*[26]

---

25  Chris Scarinzi

26  François Du Toit, Romans 8:28 Mirror Bible

Are you convinced in your heart, that because of God's love, everything that happens in your life will ultimately work out to be advantageous for you? Those who are rooted and grounded in love, have the assurance that God will work everything out to their advantage, for their best. Don't think, for a minute, that I'm saying that you will not experience pain and suffering in your walk with God! What I am saying, is that God is always working behind the scene on your behalf to bring about His desired result.

> **"Fixing our eyes on Jesus, the author and**
> **perfecter of faith,** *who for the joy set before Him*
> *endured the cross, despising the shame, and has sat*
> *down at the right hand of the throne of God."*

> *Hebrews 12:2 (NASB)*

Jesus endured the cross, so that there would be a finished product in each of us, to present to the Father.

> **"that He might present to Himself the church**
> **in all her glory,** *having no spot or wrinkle or any*
> *such thing; but that she would be holy and blameless."*

> *Ephesians 5:27 (NASB)*

When we are rooted and grounded in the love of God, then we can be confident that God wants to perfect us, even more than we would ever want to be perfected. In fact, from God's perspective, we are a finished work of grace! The Bible tells us:

> *"For by one offering **He has perfected for all time** those who are sanctified."*

*Hebrews 10:14 (NASB)*

*"The word '**perfected**' is the translation of teleioo (τελειοο), which means 'to bring to a state of completion'. Here, the completeness of the state of salvation of the believer is in view.*

*Everything essential to the salvation of the individual is included in the gift of salvation, which the sinner receives, by faith, in Messiah's sacrifice. The words 'for ever' (for all time) here are to be construed with 'perfected'. It is a permanent state of completeness in salvation to which reference is made."* [27]

*"'Making perfect' and 'making pure' are difficult to distinguish. 'Making people pure' means that God sets them apart to belong to him, or to be dedicated to him. 'Making people perfect' involves dealing completely with sin and so cleansing the conscience from guilt."* [28]

---

27  Wuest, K. S. (1997). Wuest's word studies from the Greek New Testament: for the English reader (Heb. 10:13). Grand Rapids: Eerdmans.

28  Ellingworth, P., & Nida, E. A. (1994). A handbook on the Letter to the Hebrews (p. 224). New York: United Bible Societies.

Regardless of circumstances that we encounter, while we are here on earth, we have to trust that nothing can happen to us that will not turn out for our best, and ultimately result in us being just like Jesus.

> *"Beloved, now we are children of God, and it has not appeared as yet what we will be.* **We know that when He appears, we will be like Him**, *because we will see Him just as He is."*

> *I John 3:2 (NASB)*

The bible gives an account of a time when Jesus was in the boat with His disciples, fast asleep, in the midst of a storm. In the disciples' perspective, they were fighting for their lives.

> *"They came and woke him, saying, "Lord, save us! We are perishing!"*

> *Matthew 8:25 (NASB)*

If Jesus' disciples had possessed an accurate understanding of their own identity, as well as the purpose of God for them, they would not have lost their peace over the ordeal. Something that we cannot lose sight of, is the posture of the Son; even in the midst of the storm. Jesus knew that He was loved by the Father and because of this He kept His peace, and even slept during the storm. Never do we see Jesus trying to defend, protect or comfort Himself. He was rooted and grounded in the love of

His Father, and knew that God would keep Him. Jesus found His peace in the love of the Father and was not affected by what was going on around Him. Can we trust God so much so, that we would be willing to become vulnerable in this world, knowing that God is working on our behalf even when things seem to be going wrong in our lives? God wants us to fully comprehend that no matter the circumstance, He is always at work behind the scenes for our absolute best!

> *"Yuri Gagarin is famous as the first man to fly in space. After the end of the Cold War some of Russia's cosmonauts revealed the pressures under which he operated. Gagarin's rocket ship was armed with an explosive charge, which could be detonated by radio signal. The Russians wanted to ensure Gagarin wouldn't defect by re entering earth's atmosphere anywhere but over Soviet territory. So the explosives were rigged. The charges could only be disarmed and the rocket's re-entry system activated by entering a six-digit code into the onboard system. Gagarin was given the first three numbers. The last three were to be transmitted to him just before his retrorockets were to Ore.*

> *But where the Soviet government didn't trust its cosmonauts, the head of their space program, Chief Designer Korolev did. Just before the rocket was launched Korolev pulled Gagrin aside and told him the last three numbers. Korolev had faith in Gagrin, a faith for which he was prepared to lay his job and his future on the line*

*by whispering those secret numbers. And Gagarin didn't let him down." (Source: based on an article in Popular Science, July1999.)* [29]

We can trust God with all of our hearts because He always has our best intentions, and will never fail us.

> *"Trust in the Lord with all your heart and do not lean on*
> *your own understanding. In all your ways acknowledge*
> *Him, and He will make your paths straight."*

Proverbs 3:5-6 (NASB)

Prayer Focus:

Dear heavenly Father, help me to know that You have a plan and purpose for my life, and that no matter what I am going through, You will bring about the very best result, according to Your divine plan. In Jesus' name, amen.

---

29  www.storiesforpreaching.com

# CHAPTER 9

# Motivation

MY FAMILY AND I HAD the tremendous opportunity to know a man named Dave. Dave and his wife, Sandi, were such a blessing to us in ministry, as well as personally. Dave had the most amazing ability to get people to do things. He was able to speak in such a way as to volunteer your services and yet, make you feel like it was your idea. Dave liked to call it "voluntelling." I'm pretty sure you won't find this word in the English dictionary, because Dave made it up. He had such a way about him that motivated you to help him out when he asked. Like Dave, God has His own beautiful way of motivating us to love and serve Him.

Before the end of our time together, I want us to come to the place where we have Jesus in full view, and have an accurate understanding of true motivation regarding the 'why' of loving and serving God. Motivation is defined as:

*"the reason or reasons one has for acting or behaving in a particular way."*[30]

---

30 www.googledictionary.com

The time that has been allotted to Tracy and me to raise our two children is coming to a close. Looking back over the last eighteen or so years, I reflect on the fact that our children each responded very differently, when we disciplined using the similar measures.

If we were firm toward our son with our words, he would respond in obedience, and we would not have to say anything more. Our daughter on the other hand would be offended by firm words, and respond with defiance. On the other hand, she would respond well to a soft worded correction, whereas he would fail to pick up on the subtle seriousness of such words. This is in no way meant to be critical, but to simply express my observation. We had to creatively come up with different methods of motivating our children to move in the desired direction.

Remembering back to my childhood, I can't help but recall the crazy things my brothers and I got into, while living on the farm. I was 'lucky' enough to be the middle of three of boys, and we had more than our share of energy, and spent a great deal of time outside. As you can imagine, my mom had her hands full, to keep us boys in line. Even now, I can distinctly remember a particular 'something' in the kitchen drawer, that she would pull out, when one of us was in need of some motivation. We knew that she meant business, when our eyes caught a glimpse of that rugged fourteen-inch long strap that had been cut from bailer wagon. As soon as we saw that old bailer strap, it was amazing how well behaved we would all become. There were times that each of us boys got what we had coming to us, for sure, but we never questioned our parents' love for us, and I like to think we've all turned out pretty good. Sometimes, we as parents motivate our children using fear tactics, but I can tell you that there is a more effective way. If you haven't guessed it already, the first negative motivator is fear.

Before getting married, I worked in a radiator shop for a man that seemed to have a Jekyll & Hyde personality. It seemed as though I could never predict when he would lose his temper. One morning, while soldiering the header plate of a radiator, as I had done many times before, he came up to me cursing and swearing. He proceeded to take the radiator that I was working on, and threw it on the ground. I recall being shocked to see a grown man behave in such a manner. His display of such immaturity helped me decide, right then and there, that this was the last day I would ever work for him.

A couple of years went by and he and I bumped into each other. We casually struck up a conversation. Figuring that he'd had ample time to cool down from his outburst toward me two years earlier, I felt it was appropriate for me to ask him why he had treated me that way. To this day, I'm still shocked by his reply. He told me that his goal had been to make me angry, because I worked hardest when I was angry. He used my own anger and frustration, to motivate me to work hard. That which motivates us can either be positive or negative, and will bring varied results, accordingly. No two people are wired the same, and we each respond differently to various motivators.

What I am about to express to you, I had never seen in the Bible until recently. Understanding this next passage, within the context of God's love for us, is vitally important.

> *"The oath God swore to Abraham, "To rescue us*
> *from the hand of our enemies, and* ***to enable us***
> ***to serve Him without fear*** *in holiness and*
> *righteousness before Him all the days of our lives..."*

> *Luke 1:73-75 (NASB)*

The entire law-based system was centered around a fear-based motivation. Luke speaks of what God has done, as a fulfillment of the promise He made to Abraham, enabling us to serve God without fear. No longer do we have to have fear as the motivator for our serving and loving Him. The Apostle John also writes concerning this principle:

> ***"There is no fear in love***; *but perfect love casts*
> *out fear, because fear involves punishment, and*
> *the one who fears is not perfected in love."*

> *I John 4:18 (NASB)*

The only way that the people could serve God without fear was to have the consequences of failure removed. We covered this in chapter two on fear, but this is closely related, so some of this bears repeating. We know that He, who knew no sin, became sin for us, taking on the full weight of God's wrath, for our sins, thereby declaring us righteous. The reason we can approach God without fear, is He removed sin, and with it, the fear of punishment.

Part of approaching God, is how we serve Him. The servant that is motivated by fear, will serve with a slave mindset, living in fear of coming up short, and disappointing the master. In contrast, the one who is rooted and grounded in the love of God serves with confidence in God's approval.

> *"For God so loved the world, that He gave His only begotten Son, that whoever believes in Him shall not perish, but have eternal life. For **God did not send the Son into the world to judge the world, but that the world might be saved through Him**."*

> *John 3:16-17 (NASB)*

Does this passage in any way suggest that God sent His Son into the world to motivate the world to serve Him by fear? Fear will never produce lasting results! Motivating someone through fear may give the illusion of result, but I can assure you that there will be a season of rebellion sooner or later, where they will fight to get out from under the grip of fear. Fear based motivation will not produce results that last, but we can see that abiding in love produces fruit that will endure.

*"If you abide in Me, and My words abide in
you, ask whatever you wish, and it will be
done for you. My Father is glori4ed by this,
that you bear much fruit, and so prove to be
My disciples. Just as the Father has loved Me,
I have also loved you; abide in My love."*

*John 15:7-9 (NASB)*

*""And the one also who had received the one talent
came up and said, 'Master, I knew you to be a
hard man, reaping where you did not sow and
gathering where you scattered no seed. And **I was
afraid, and went away and hid your talent
in the ground**. See, you have what is yours.'"*

*Matthew 25:24-25 (NASB)*

The servant that was living in fear of his master's judgment produced the least fruit. God did not send His son so that we would be motivated by fear, as it was in the days of the law, but that our motivation for loving and serving Him would change. God removed from us, the punishment of sin, by taking it upon himself. Let us not rob ourselves by operating out of a fear-based motivation, as we serve Him. We are, as Isaiah declared, able to serve Him without fear, but in holiness and righteousness. If we comprehend and receive the simple fact that our sin was removed from us, along with the punishment, and that we have been made holy and righteous, there is nothing left for us to do, but to love God.

> *"Therefore, my brethren, you also were made to die to the Law through the body of Christ,* **so that you might be joined to another,** *to Him who was raised from the dead, in order* **that we might bear fruit for God."**

Romans 7:4 (NASB)

You have died to the fear of not fulfilling the requirements of the law, so that you can go and bear fruit. How do we accomplish this? We bear fruit by simply abiding in the love of God in Christ.

There is another motivator that we need to guard our hearts against, and that is doing for the sake of a reward. There is nothing wrong with a reward, but if the underlying motivation is in any way self-seeking, then we are not serving out of love for God.

When reward is the motivator, when working with children, for instance, then you will always be struggling to coming up with new rewards to keep them motivated. Is there a hidden heart issue being revealed when we perform for the reward? What if your reward only comes at the end of this life? You may get tired before you get your reward and stop performing. It seems to me that this is where much of the church is at. God's word certainly promises us rewards for faithful service in this life, but let's not lose the heart for why we serve.

Once again, written in the Bible, is the most powerful motivator for us who believe, and it's found in the simplicity of the Gospel message.

> ""For **God so loved** the world, **that He gave**
> His only begotten Son, that whoever believes in
> Him shall not perish, but have eternal life."

*John 3:16 (NASB)*

> "By this the love of God was manifested in us, that God
> has sent His only begotten Son into the world so that
> we might live through Him. In this is love, not that
> we loved God, but that He loved us and sent His Son
> to be the propitiation for our sins. Beloved, **if God so
> loved** us, **we also ought to love** one another."

*I John 4:9-11 (NASB)*

> "**We love, because He first loved** us."

*I John 4:19 (NASB)*

What motivated God to send Jesus Christ? The answer, my friend, is love. New Covenant motivation is only through the finished work of Christ on the cross: Love expressing itself through faith. We love, we believe, and then we do! If you are still caught up in fear motivation, where you feel that God will be angry if you don't give or serve, let it go right now. When you look at Him, you will begin to reflect His love freely as it was given to you, and you will, in turn, give it to others. If you are motivated by someday getting a reward, your reason for serving, is self-seeking. Look at Jesus, and love Him, and the rewards will come, and then your motive for serving will be pure. As we abide, and draw close to Jesus, His love will compel us to act! This is the motivation of our faith, as we are rooted and grounded in love.

> *"Faith is not something we do to get God to do something back to us; faith is what happens to us when we realize what God has already done for us."* [31]

Prayer Focus:
Dear heavenly Father, I pray that you would help me to see that it is because of your love toward me, that my motivation for loving you, is possible. Help me to guard my heart from wrong motivation for loving and serving you. In Jesus' name, Amen!

---

31  Francois Du Toit

## FINAL THOUGHTS

ONE DAY, I WAS ASKED to lead a bible study in the morning portion of a conference being held in Slave Lake, Alberta, Canada. In the morning of the meeting, while I was in prayer, the Lord showed me, in my spirit, the name of a lady. The lady's name was a common one, but it was spelled in a very peculiar way. I proceeded to tell the attendees that while in prayer, God had given me a word for a lady, and the name was common, but the spelling was unusual. When I called out the lady's name, there was a girl in the crowd who responded with tears streaming down her face. Her name was spelled just like the Lord had shown me, and I encouraged her with the word of the Lord. She had been praying that morning, feeling completely insignificant and wondering if God ever thought about her, and if she had any importance or worth.

Just think about the fact that God spoke her name to me at that moment, and spelled it out, so that there would be no mistake. Of all the people on the face of the planet, God turned His face toward her, in her moment of desperation to let her know how special she was to Him. David A. Powlison writes:

*"The love of Christ for me will get last say. He is merciful to me for his name's sake, for the sake of his own goodness, for the sake of his stead- fast love and compassion (Psalm 25). When he thinks about me, he remembers what he is like, and that is my exceeding joy.*

*My indestructible hope is that he has turned his face towards me, and he will never turn away."* [32]

God wants each and every one of us to know that His heart is lovingly, and continually turned toward us. He is always ready, each and every day, to strongly support, encourage, empower and love us completely and unconditionally.

*"For the eyes of the Lord move to and fro throughout the earth so that He may support those whose heart is completely His."*

II Chronicles 16:9 (NASB)

*"At best we are but clay, animated dust; but viewed as sinners, we are monsters indeed. Let it be published in heaven as a miracle that the Lord Jesus should set His heart's love upon people like us."* [33]

---

32  David A. Powlison

33  Alistair Begg

Perhaps you are like me, and you are amazed at the wonder that God would ever want to look your direction, and set His heart toward you, to show you His love continually. Our attitude needs to shift from feeling unworthy, to accepting the fact that we have been made worthy. We need to develop a 'much more' mindset of how God thinks and feels toward us.

> *"Now to Him who is able to do far more*
> *abundantly beyond all that we ask or think,*
> *according to the power that works within us,"*

*Ephesians 3:20 (NASB)*

God has limitless grace to empower our lives, but we have to make the shift in our thinking, in order to receive it. In closing, this is my prayer for you, that you would experience the 'much more' reality that belongs to you as a son of God. It is my heart's desire, that the lessons in this book have been a blessing for you, and will continue to serve you, as you allow God to show you His love on a daily basis.

# ABOUT THE AUTHOR

RODNEY LIVES IN DRAYTON VALLEY, Alberta Canada with His wife Tracy and two children Graham and Rachel. Together, Tracy and Rodney have been pastors and traveling itinerant ministers since 1996. Their ministry is called Resounding Word Ministries International, and their mission is to "Equip the Nations One Person at a Time". Their vision is releasing the resounding word of the Lord to the nations through preaching and teaching that helps removes the stones in peoples' thinking, thereby enabling them to see Jesus and experience abundant life transformation (Isaiah 62:10).

## OUR EXPERIENCE

- Ordained P.A.O.C.
- B.R.E Degree / Pastoral Major
- 21 Years of Pastoral Ministry
- 14 Years of International Ministry

- (Europe, Asia, USA, Mexico)
- 20 Years of Camp Ministry (All Ages)
- 20 Years of Children's Ministry
- Church Planting
- Leadership Training
- Mission Team Leading

## WHAT CAN OUR MINISTRY DO FOR YOUR CHURCH, MINISTRY OR EVENT?
### PREACHING / TEACHING

In our ministry, we listen and hear what God is saying for each church and event and only minister as He is leading. We operate in the gifts of the Holy Spirit as God leads and empowers us in order to help people see that the ministry we do is from God and not from ourselves. Some of the things that we offer though our ministry:

- Local Church Services (Midweek / Sunday Meetings)
- Evangelistic Crusades
- Conference Speaking
- Youth / Children's Meetings
- Small Groups
- Summer Camp Speaking
- Listening Prayer Counseling
- Compassion Canada Representative

# TRAINING WORKSHOPS

- Children's Ministry
- Healing School
- New Creation Realities
- Life Groups
- Missions
- Worship
- Leadership

## RODZILLA KID / FAMILY SHOWS

We offer a proven quality family show that is guaranteed to entertain all audiences making for a memorable event. We have entertained children and families all over the world, making them laugh out loud and helping them see Jesus in a real way. We use illusion, ventriloquism, music and other great skills to engage our generation with the gospel message. This ministry is very effective for the following situations:

- School Assemblies
- AWANA Groups
- Children / Youth Meetings
- Kids / Youth Camps
- Christmas Parties
- Special Events

## TEAM MISSION ENCOUNTERS

We have been leading Mission Teams since 1999 and have had projects in Europe, Asia and Mexico. We would love the opportunity to help your church plan a mission excursion to one of several amazing locations in the world where your people can experience the mission field first hand. **MAXIMIZING OUR MINISTRY IN YOUR CHURCH** Some churches like to combine several elements into a weekend of ministry that can touch the whole church as well as the community. **For example**: A Friday afternoon school performance sponsored by the local church to bless the school along with a Friday night youth meeting,

Saturday workshop for children's ministry leaders to help develop their ministry skills and a meeting with an evangelist preacher and teacher on Sunday morning.

## BOOKING

Booking our ministry is as simple as choosing a date that works for you and connect with us by pressing the link on the home page. We will do our absolute best to work with you to make your event the best it can be.

## FINANCE

In our ministry, we travel by faith in God & his Word which says: "And my God will supply all your needs according to His riches in glory in Christ Jesus." (Philippians 4:19)

We believe that God will supply our needs, whether it is day-to-day living expenses or ministry related expenses. Our common practice is to minister for a free will love offering, or dis- cuss honorariums with the directors of Camps, Conferences or other ministry outreaches.

**Web Site**: www.resoundingword.org
**CONTACT INFORMATION**:
Rodney & Tracy Fortin General Delivery
Drayton Valley, AB T7A 1T1
**Email**: zillasworld_mission@hotmail.com

## Chapter 1 – Roots

**Scriptures:** Ephesians 3:14-19; Colossians 2:6-7; John 15:1-8; Romans

8:35-39; Romans 8:11; John 14:26; I John 4:8; I John 4:19; Proverbs 12:3

### Questions for Study

What is the purpose of the root system of the tree, and how does this relate to us as believers in Jesus Christ?

What is the evidence that love has taken root in our lives? How does God support us?

What does our transformation depend on?

## Chapter 2 – Worth

**Scriptures:** Genesis 1:26-27; Genesis 2:7; John 17:20-21; Psalm 139; Isaiah 59:2; John 3:16; Matthew 20:28; I Timothy 2:5-6; I Corinthians 6:19-20; Romans 5:8; Matthew 3:17; John 15:9; Ephesians 1:6; Romans 8:38-39

## Questions for Study
How do we determine the value of something?

Who is the one responsible to set a value on us?

Why is it that we begin our life devalued instead of knowing our worth?

In what truth is our entire identity and value is hidden?

What was the price that God used to determine our worth?

## Chapter 3 – Fearless
**Scriptures:** I John 4:18; Romans 3:23; Romans 6:23; Ephesians 3:11-12; II Corinthians 5:21; Isaiah 53:5; John 3:36; I John 2:2; Isaiah 53:10; Romans 8:15-16; I John 4:18; Romans 4:8

## Questions for Study
What does the expectation of punishment do in our relationship with God?

What happens when the punishment is removed?

How have we been given confident access to come to God without fear?

What does it mean to you, that your sins have been removed?

## Chapter 4 – Giver
**Scriptures:** Galatians 3:1-9; John 3:16; Ephesians 2:8-9; Romans 11:6; Hebrews 12:2; Galatians 3:3; Hebrews 10:14; II Corinthians 3:16-18; Galatians 3:4-5; John 6:63; John 6:28-29; II Corinthians 5:21; I John 4:8; I John 4:19

## Questions for Study

What does it mean to have a performance-based relationship with God?

Who is the initiator of giving in our relationship with God?

Explain the process of attaining a righteous standing before God.

Did we do anything to earn righteous standing before God?

Why does God give anything to us?

What is one word that defines the character of God that is an absolute truth?

## Chapter 5 – Provide

**Scriptures:** Philippians 4:6; Matthew 6:25-34; Luke 11:9-13; James 4:2; Philippians 4:19

## Questions for Study

What is the reason we don't have what we need?

How do the words, "how much more" demonstrate the heart of the Father?

## Chapter 6 – Knowing

**Scriptures:** Hebrews 10:24; I Corinthians 2:4-5; Habakkuk 2:14; Hebrews 1:1-3; Isaiah 11:1-3; John 5:19-20; I Corinthians 2:6-16; I Corinthians 2:12-13; I Corinthians 14:2; John 5:20; Galatians 4:6; I John 3:1; Jeremiah 33:3

## Questions for Study

What does the world need to see from us to know we are truly from God?

What conclusion did the blasts of wind bring us to?

What is the reason God speaks to us?

What are the hidden mysteries and how can we know them? Who are the sons of God?

## Chapter 7 – Near
**Scriptures:** Matthew 1:23; Matthew 28:20; Mark 16:19-20; Joshua 1:9; Isaiah 41:10; Deuteronomy 31:6; John 3:1-2; I Corinthians 2:3-5; Psalm 145:18

## Questions for Study
Why is there confidence in knowing that we are not alone?

What does it mean when it says; "The Lord worked with them?"

What does it mean that the love of God affirms His presence with us?

How does the world know that God is with us?

What is a main factor that shows that God is with us?

## Chapter 8 – Goodness
**Scriptures:** Romans 8:28; Hebrews 12:2; Ephesians 5:27; Hebrews 10:14; I John 3:2; Matthew 8:25; Proverbs 3:5-6

## Questions for Study
What happens when we have a need and we chose to sit down?

What does it mean that God works things for our good?

According to Hebrews 10:14 we have been made perfect, does this mean we can't sin?

What is the main reason why we can trust God with our lives?

## Chapter 9 – Motivation

Scriptures: Luke 1:73-75; I John 4:18; John 3:16-17; John 15:7-9; Matthew 24:24-25; Romans 7:4; John 3:16; I John 4:9-11; I John 4:19;

## Questions for Study

What are the two wrong reasons for serving and loving God?

What can we do in our lives to produce lasting fruit for God?

What should our motivation be for why we love and serve God?

Made in the USA
Charleston, SC
15 February 2017